The Seven P's of Brillian

Also in this series

Also by Sue Cowley

The Seven P's of Brilliant Voice Usage

SUE COWLEY

Sue Cowley Books Ltd

2013

Sue Cowley Books Ltd
PO Box 1172
Bristol BS39 4ZJ

www.suecowley.co.uk

First published 2013

Part of the 'Alphabet Sevens' Series

Also in this series:

The Seven C's of Positive Behaviour Management
The Seven T's of Practical Differentiation

ISBN: 978-1489538024

Contents

Introduction

As a teacher, you are a 'professional voice user': your voice is crucial in allowing you to fulfil your day-to-day classroom role. It's surprising, then, how little attention we give to effective voice usage as a profession. The way that you use your voice will impact on pretty much every aspect of your teaching: how your children perceive you, how quickly they learn, how effectively you manage your class, how well your students behave, how engaged they are. As well as learning how to use your voice brilliantly, you must also understand how to protect it, because you must use it every day of your working life. This concise guide to voice usage will help you learn how to do all this and much more.

I'm always amazed at how many teachers tell me they have received little or no training in how to use their voices, so I've written this guide to bridge that gap. In this book I offer you practical and straightforward advice about using your voice more effectively in your classroom. The strategies and techniques that I give here will help you to improve the sound and quality of your verbal communication, to understand how your voice works, and also how you can protect it from damage.

If you think back to when you were a schoolchild, I'm sure you can bring to mind the voices of some of your teachers. I have memories from my own school days of various different vocal sounds. There were those teachers whose voices sounded harsh, or stressed, or screechy, or bland: I found it really hard to listen to and learn from those teachers. Then there were those teachers who had gentle, or expressive, or melodious, or passionate voices: those were the teachers who made learning come to life for me. The way that you talk to your children will have a huge influence on their chances of success within your classroom.

Remember, every time you speak in your classroom, you model voice and language usage for your students. If you get it right, they will learn how to use their voices in a clear, eloquent, expressive and creative manner. They will come to understand that our words, and our voices, allow us to share our ideas, opinions, feelings and thoughts with the world. Your students will listen to how you speak to them then they will model their own approaches at least partly on what you do.

The ideas in this book are ones that you can use immediately, both to improve the quality of your teaching, and also to enhance your classroom management skills. You will find exercises to try out throughout the book, designed to help you consider and improve your voice usage (look for the words 'TRY THIS'). You owe it to yourself, and to your students, to do everything you can to use your voice well, and to protect it from harm. This book will help you become an effective, creative and downright *brilliant* classroom communicator.

Sue Cowley
www.suecowley.co.uk

The First P:

Prosody

The First P: Prosody

The word 'prosody' describes the way that your voice sounds: the 'music' and 'personality' of your vocal sound, if you will. Prosody includes the rhythms, stresses, pitches, inflections and intonations within your vocal sound, and is sometimes referred to as 'tone of voice'. When combined with your own particular physical make-up, these aspects of voice usage create a voice that is uniquely yours, one that friends and family will recognise instantly.

You can vary the prosody of your voice according to the situation you're in, or the meaning or feelings you want to communicate. This is one of the key skills of the highly effective teacher – that ability to adapt what you do to suit your class. Your children will gauge what kind of person/teacher you are by the sound your voice makes. Ideally, you want to create a varied and engaging vocal sound: one that hooks them in, holds their interest and attention and helps them understand and learn.

By creating a high quality vocal sound, you will help your students learn how to listen properly and you will also motivate them to learn more effectively. For instance, if the teacher uses an enthusiastic sound, full of wonder, this encourages the students to pay attention and to feel passionate about a subject or topic. Where the teacher uses a quiet, curious sound, this encourages the students to listen hard and to take an interest in what is being said.

TRY THIS: Think about a variety of different people that you watch on the television: some whose voices you really like to listen to, others whose voices you find irritating or off-putting. Consider why you feel positive or negative about these people – what is it about their voices that draws you in, or pushes you away?

Effective Use of Tone

Tone is sometimes referred to as 'emotional prosody'. In other words, tone is those vocal sounds that we use to communicate messages about our emotional, intellectual or psychological state. Often we do this instinctively – our voice naturally mirrors our internal state. But teachers need to do much more than this with tone of voice, because our voices are so important in managing both learning and behaviour. We need to make conscious decisions about how we want or need to sound in order to make learning happen or to control a class. Then we must learn how to create and maintain that sound within our voices, even under the most stressful of conditions.

Teachers who make effective use of tone are able to communicate their feelings or wishes to a class through the vocal sound they use, as well as through the vocabulary they choose. Your tone of voice will help your children understand a whole host of different things: that you are interested in what they have to say, or curious about their ideas, or happy to see them, or wondering why they are still talking, or perhaps that you simply want them to calm down.

In teaching it's often the case that you don't *want* your voice to mirror how you feel inside. Because inside you might be feeling terrified, or stressed, or really irritated, and you don't want to let your class know that. But of course you don't have to let every emotion show through your vocal sound, just as you don't have to actually feel an emotion to put that particular tone into your voice. Some days you might not feel all that curious, or happy, or interested, or whatever emotion it is that you need to get across to be an effective teacher. However you can still make your voice *sound* curious, or happy, or interested, even if you're not feeling that way at that precise moment in time.

There's a lot more to tone than meets the eye (or rather, the ear). Here are some points and ideas for you to consider:

✓ Children use a variety of clues and cues to gather meaning from spoken language. It's not just about the words you use; it's got a great deal to do with the way you sound (and look) as well.

✓ The less spoken English a child has, the more they will rely on the *sound* of what you are saying. This means that very young children, and also those children who have English as an additional language (EAL), will rely a great deal on tone to pick up meaning.

✓ Think about how people respond to spoken language when they travel abroad. They tend to home in on factors other than vocabulary to gather meaning. So, you might look at the context, the person's facial expressions, any gestures they are using, and their tone of voice. This is what children with limited spoken English skills will be doing in your classroom, in an attempt to gather meaning from what you say.

✓ Your students' learning and behaviour is affected by the way that they read your emotional state. If they feel you are confident and enthusiastic, this will encourage them to focus and pay attention. If they perceive you as bored and disinterested, this will discourage them from working hard for you. A huge part of the way that the students read your emotions is to do with how your voice sounds to them.

✓ The more tone you put into your voice, the more you will adapt your facial expressions to match that sound.

The more you use facial expressions, the better your students will engage with and respond to you.

✓ We use the right side of our brains to judge the tone of someone's voice, and to figure out what emotions they are feeling. This is the side of the brain linked to creativity, emotions and intuition.

✓ Research has shown that the voice-sensitive brain regions are activated very early in a child's life (at around 7 months). It seems that our tone of voice can trigger the parts of the brain that help children understand a speaker's emotional state. Tone of voice is therefore a key factor in helping children develop empathy for others.

✓ As well as thinking about the tone you use, learn to pick up on what your students' vocal tone is telling you about *their* emotional states.

Teacher Tone

The kind of vocal tone you choose to use will depend on a number of factors: your own personality and your beliefs about teaching, the age and 'type' of students you work with, and the kind of area where you teach. For young and well-motivated students, a 'teacher-y' voice works well. This is a firm, clear yet caring tone. The children understand that you want the best for them, but that at the same time you will be able to maintain calm and order in a class of children.

For older or very challenging students, it's best to aim for a more natural sounding voice – nothing too 'teacher-y' or strident. This will help you avoid potential tensions or conflicts, because the students will see you as being 'on the level' with them, rather than trying to be authoritarian, and place yourself above them. It's a tricky balance to achieve, because you don't want to sound like you're trying to be their friend, rather that you are speaking to them on a mature and adult level.

Here are some of my top tips for using tone effectively with your students:

- ✓ Go slightly over the top with your vocal tone – go just a little bit further than feels natural, especially if you are new to teaching. The younger the children you teach, the more exaggerated you should make your tone.

- ✓ Experiment with tone: see how you can use it to get your children excited, and equally how you can use it to calm them down. Imagine your voice as being like a musical instrument – you can play a fast, happy tune to get everyone moving, but you can also play a slow, calming and restful tune to quieten things down.

- ✓ Don't overdo tone if you're teaching older students or adults. You have to pitch it right or they may 'read' your tone as being patronising. Incorporate more tone in a subtle way.

- ✓ With older students, focus at first on creating a tone that shows how *you* are feeling. For instance, you might say 'I'm really excited about this part of the topic'. This is less threatening than tone related to the students' learning, because it's about your feelings rather than theirs. (For example, if you said 'That's a *great* piece of work' they might find it patronising or embarrassing.)

- ✓ Learn to 'step outside' of yourself, and to hear what you sound like from your children's perspective. If you find this hard, record or film yourself teaching, and listen back to it. Brace yourself before you play the recording – most people sound very different in reality to how they imagine they sound.

TRY THIS: Film yourself doing some whole class teaching, for about ten minutes or so. Listen once to the recording without looking at the images. What do you notice about how your voice sounds? How would you feel as a student, listening to a teacher with this kind of voice? Now watch the recording, but with the sound turned down. What do you notice about how your face and body contribute to the students' levels of understanding? How does your body support what your voice is saying?

The Tonal Toolkit

You can of course create different tones in your voice, through using your physicality. By making various different facial expressions and movements, you help yourself learn how to make different sounds as well. Here are some ideas to get you thinking about how you can do this:

✓ Curiosity - screw up your forehead and start what you say with 'hmm' or 'umm'. Squish your lips together and create a questioning sound in your voice.

✓ Interest - raise both eyebrows and focus intently on what the student is saying to you, making continual eye contact. Start what you say with pursed lips and an 'ooo' sound.

✓ Surprise - open your mouth and take in a sharp breath before speaking. Raise your eyebrows and open your eyes wide.

✓ Enthusiasm – lean in towards the person you are addressing, and widen your mouth to show excitement and energy.

TRY THIS: Experiment with tone by trying this simple exercise. Say the phrase 'tomato ketchup' several times, in a dull, flat monotone. Now say the phrase again, but this time say it as though you are telling a friend the most exciting thing in the world. What was the difference

9

between the two? Did you notice yourself using more facial expressions and body language when you put excitement into your tone? Can you transfer this feeling over into the way you talk in your classroom?

Pitch of Voice

Your 'pitch' of voice – how high or low it sounds – is all part of the prosody of your voice. Pitch is created by the speed at which the vocal folds vibrate. As the number of vibrations increases, the voice sounds higher; as the number of vibrations decreases, the voice sounds lower. Female teachers typically have higher pitched voices than their male counterparts. This is because women's vocal folds tend to be shorter and consequently the folds vibrate more frequently when a female teacher is speaking.

It's important to understand how pitch works, and to be able to control the pitch of your voice, because differences in pitch will have an immediate impact on your students. Your students will subconsciously use the pitch of your voice to help them judge you and your teaching style.

Here are some ideas to consider about your use of pitch:

✓ Our voices tend to rise in pitch when we become frightened, because the muscles around the voice box contract.

✓ When you are feeling tense, you are also likely to stop breathing in a relaxed way. Again, this can make the pitch of your voice start to rise.

✓ Your children may pick up on a gradually rising pitch of voice, as a signal that you are worried or that you feel you are losing control. An overly high pitch suggests stress, tension and fear. It also tends to sound quite funny from the children's perspective.

✓ When you find yourself feeling tense, check your body, neck and face for muscular stress and take several breaths *before* you begin to speak. This will help you find the right vocal pitch and tone to calm yourself and your class.

✓ Remember that your voice can also rise in pitch for positive reasons. It rises when you are excited, so a high-pitched voice can be used to create a lively, happy feeling for your children.

✓ A rising pitch is also useful when you are asking questions – end the question on a slightly higher note. This gives a curious sound and will encourage your students to respond.

✓ Teachers sometimes mistake a higher pitch for a louder sound. Remember: just because you raise the level of pitch of your voice, this doesn't make your voice sound any louder to your children.

✓ A low pitch of voice can suggest calm, authority and relaxation. Aim for the lower end of the pitch range within your own voice, when you need to calm down or control your students.

Try this: Say the words below one after the other, aiming for a high pitch as you say the first word, and a low pitch as you say the second. Consider the differences in the way that your voice sounds, and in how you make the high or low-pitched sounds:

* *High/Low*
* *Up/Down*
* *Ping/Pong*
* *Ding/Dong*
* *Light/Dark*
* *Top/Bottom*

The Second P:

Pace

The Second P: Pace

It's tempting to believe that if you speak more quickly, you will get more learning done with your children: that you will simply fit more into your lessons. However, if you speak *too* quickly, your children will not understand what you are saying. What you're after is *variety* of pace, so that the speed of what you say changes according to what you are trying to achieve with your class.

You should always think of using your voice in the context of understanding – i.e. how can I make sure that my children understand what I am saying? Children's auditory systems are not fully developed until about the age of fifteen: young children simply do not process sound as well as older children or adults. They need you to speak more slowly and clearly so that they have more time to make sense of what you say.

Think of words as being a bit like pieces of chewing gum: you can stretch them out, you can chew them up, you can play around with the way that they sound. You might use short, clipped staccato chews on the gum when giving a firm instruction. You could use long, drawn out pulls of the gum when you are elucidating on the finer points of your subject. You might even spit figurative bits of gum at your class to make a firm point with them.

Vocal pace, whether fast or slow, is created by:

✓ The speed of your voice – how quickly you actually speak.
✓ The speed of each of the individual words as you say them – whether you draw some out to sound longer, or give others a short, attacking feel.

✓ Any spaces you leave *in between* the words, for instance taking a pause to aid the students' understanding or to ensure that you have the class's attention.
✓ The individual words you use – short, single syllable words make for a faster pace, because you can say them more quickly and easily.
✓ The type of words you use – if you use a lot of complex, hard to pronounce words, this will inevitably slow down the speed of your speech.
✓ The way that you construct your sentences – long or short sentences, extended clauses or simple constructions, complex linguistic features or basic vocabulary – all can help to create different kinds of vocal pace.

If you enjoy reading thrillers, you might have noticed how an author will use short sentences and mainly single syllable words to create a sense of pace, excitement and forward motion. Have a think about the difference between this:

"Toby sped down the hall. The gunman was close behind him. He could hear his breath. Smell his sweat. Sense that he was there. Toby's heart thumped hard in his chest. Bang, bang, bang."

And this:

"Toby ran quickly along the corridor, followed closely by the murderous gunman. Toby could hear the gunman's heavy breathing, and he could smell the acrid scent of his sweating body in the air all around him. Inside his chest, he could feel the thump-thumping of his heart as fear flooded through his entire body."

Notice how the first example has a choppy, staccato feel to it, while the second has a smoother, flowing feel. As a teacher, you can achieve similar effects through the vocabulary and language construction that you use in your classroom.

Pace and Learning

The way that you pace your language can boost the learning that happens within your classroom. By giving pace to your voice, you create a sense of motivation and forward momentum within a lesson. At the same time, balance that forwards movement with time for the children to reinforce learning or assimilate ideas. A slow pace is very useful for in-depth thinking and detailed responses.

My top tips for vocal pace and learning are to:

✓ Give linguistic 'cues' for learning, to help your children pace their learning behaviours. For instance, you might say 'when I say go ...' before you give a set of instructions, to ensure that the children wait for you to finish your instructions before they begin.

✓ Use a slow pace to give instructions, so that the students have time to assimilate what you are saying. Use clear, simple language to ensure understanding.

✓ When you ask a question, incorporate a pause at the end to give students time to think about their answers.

✓ When a student gives a particularly good suggestion or thought, 'pounce' on it by using a slightly quicker pace to show that you believe it has merit.

✓ Draw out the pace a bit when you are thinking about a question, to show how your own thought processes take time. So you might slow down to say: 'Hmmm, yes I can see why you might think that but ...'.

✓ Use a faster pace when you want to give a sense of excitement to a subject. Incorporate tone as well to really boost your students' perception of how interesting a topic is.

As well as pacing the individual words, consider how the *type* of vocabulary you use will affect the pace of speech and of learning. Aim to offer two kinds of words: simple, readily understandable ones for clarity, and longer, more complex ones for higher order thinking. It's very useful to say the same thing twice: once in a simple way for the less able or EAL students, and a second time for the most able, using more complex vocabulary or sentence constructions to stretch their understanding.

Pace and Behaviour

You can also use the pace of your voice as part of your classroom and behaviour management systems. By changing the pace of your voice, you can calm a class down or alternatively rev them up into a frenzy of excitement. This effect is particularly pronounced with younger children, who are very responsive to the energy and pace within a teacher's voice.

Remember that a slower pace gives thinking time, and it allows a child to assimilate what you are saying. You should slow down the speed of your voice when you:

✓ need to calm the children down and regain their focus and attention;
✓ are talking to a child about the choices they have around behaviour;
✓ are explaining what the consequences of a particular misbehaviour will be;

✓ need the whole class to pay attention, for instance counting down from ten to zero, starting fairly fast, but gradually getting slower and slower as you reach the end of your countdown.

The Power of the Pause

Teachers should never under estimate how powerful a pause can be within a busy classroom. It's tempting to want to fill all the space with noise – almost as though this will prove that learning is happening within your lesson. It's also tempting to want to use your voice to pull the class to you when you need their attention, because it feels wrong somehow to simply watch and wait. But pauses, and the silent spaces they create, have huge benefits both for you and for your children.

Pauses are important and useful because:

✓ A pause suggests a sense of teacher relaxation and confidence – you don't feel the need to fill all the space with noise because you feel in control of the situation already.

✓ Pausing gives you a chance to rest your voice during the busy teaching day, and it gives you a moment to breathe deeply. Hopefully, you will feel able to relax within the silent pause as well.

✓ You can use pauses (along with the appropriate non-verbal signals) to show to the class that you are waiting. They learn to read your body language, and begin to understand that behaviour is a two-way street. It's not all about you forcing them to behave; it's also about them choosing to do so.

✓ A pause will encourage the children to bring their attention to you, rather than you always having to call for them to listen. This helps the students learn to take responsibility for their own behaviour.

✓ Over time, teacher pauses push the students to develop self-discipline and the ability to focus, as they bring themselves to you. These are key skills that they need in order to pay attention to spoken language.

✓ The space between one bit of speaking and the next gives your children time to assimilate, think about and understand what you have been saying.

✓ Calm, and silence, are key components in allowing children to focus and to learn effectively. Don't feel that you always have to chatter away, or that your students do, either.

The Third P:

Pronunciation

The Third P: Pronunciation

The teacher's pronunciation will affect whether the students can hear and understand what is being said. If the teacher mutters or runs his or her words together, the children will obviously struggle to even hear, let alone understand. The teacher's pronunciation also has an impact on the meaning the students extract from what is being said. The way the teacher pronounces or emphasises different words within a sentence can significantly change the meaning that is implied or extracted from those words.

However, this is most definitely *not* to say that you have to speak in a 'posh' voice, or that you should hide your natural accent. Rather, it is to say that you have to pronounce the individual words clearly, so that they are easy to understand. The important thing to consider is clarity of pronunciation, rather than worrying about the kind of sound you actually make.

Mirroring

Many teachers pick up on and begin to emulate the vocal sounds that they hear from their students. This is often done subconsciously, although there are some teachers who like to pick up and use the local accent in a more conscious manner. By very slightly mirroring your students' pronunciation, you can help them connect with you, relate to you and feel included. It's a subtle technique, and you must not go too far with it or it threatens to turn into parody. Again, I must emphasise that this is not about copying young people's slang or jargon, or about encouraging you to use poor pronunciation. Rather, it's about creating a very slight echo of the children's vocal sound within your own voice.

For instance, when I taught in London (where I was born and raised), I could sometimes hear my own tendency to emphasise the 'London-ness' of my accent. This happened particularly when I was dealing with the more challenging students, who I felt would connect better with me if I didn't sound too far removed from their world.

When I moved to teach overseas, I had to downplay this London quality and use a more generic, Received Pronunciation type of accent instead. This helped the students with EAL to understand me clearly and it also allowed them to learn English without any particular regional accent. Similarly, when I taught in Bristol, it wasn't long before I started mirroring (just slightly) the West Country accent of my students.

If you have a very strong regional or native accent, and you are teaching well outside of the area where you were brought up, you may need to be especially careful with pronunciation. Once again, this is *not* to say that you should change your accent, but rather that you should be aware of any words that, with your particular accent, are especially difficult to hear. The key question to ask is: 'Can my students understand exactly what I'm saying?'

Vowel and Consonant Sounds

Within speech, there are two types of sounds – vowel sounds and consonant sounds. It's worth thinking in detail about how you form these different sounds, because this will help you achieve the very best pronunciation. Speaking is very much a physical activity. Much of the time we are completely unaware of the physicality of our speech, because we do it so naturally. When you become more conscious of the physical act of creating different sounds, it helps you focus on the mechanics of how it is done properly.

Vowel sounds:

✓ These are formed when you shape your mouth with your tongue and your lips.
✓ Your teeth are not involved in creating vowel sounds and your tongue does not 'hit' any part of the inside of your mouth.
✓ Vowel sounds help your voice to carry across a room. (Think of what happens when you call out the sounds 'eh' or 'oy'.)
✓ Apparently, the word 'ahoy' (which nowadays we associate with children's pirate shows on TV), was originally used by sailors because it carried so well across open water.
✓ As you make a vowel sound, you should be able to feel the breath/sound reverberating in the spaces within your head. (Try the exercise below to get a feel for this effect.)

TRY THIS: *Make these sounds, one after the other, holding the vowel sound at the end for as long as you can on one breath: mmmooooooooo, mmmeeeeeee, mmmaaaaaaa, mmmuuuuuu. As you make each vowel sound, think about what happens to your mouth — what different shapes does it make as the vowel sound changes? Can you feel the vowel sound vibrating within the spaces inside your skull?*

Consonant sounds:

✓ These sounds are made when you use your tongue, teeth and lips in various combinations.

✓ To create each consonant sound, your tongue, teeth or lips will come together in some way – bouncing, banging, pressing, pushing, flicking, etc.

✓ For instance: to make a 'p' sound, your lips bounce off each other, whereas to make a 'l' sound, your tongue curls against the roof of your mouth and then flicks out.

✓ Consonant sounds help make your words sound clear to a listener.

✓ The more clearly you pronounce your consonants, the better your students will be able to hear what you say.

✓ The more precise and physical you are with the muscular movements, the clearer the consonant sounds will be. (See below for an activity that explores how different consonant sounds are made.)

TRY THIS: Work your way through the alphabet, pronouncing the sound that the letter can make within a word, rather than saying the letters themselves. So, you would say 'Ahh' rather than 'A', 'Buh' rather than 'B', and so on. As you say each letter sound, focus on the part of your mouth that you are using. Is it your tongue, lips, teeth and in what combination/place? Sometimes it will be your tongue pushing against the roof of your mouth ('tuh'), other times it will be your lips pushing together ('buh'). Identify the physical movement for each sound, being as precise as possible about how you actually make that sound.

Hard Attack/Easy Onset

When you're working on precise pronunciation, take care to avoid what voice therapists call the 'hard attack'. This is when you bring your vocal folds together with too much force, and it is potentially damaging to your voice. You will typically perform this 'hard attack' on vowel sounds rather than consonants.

25

Try saying the following sentence: 'Apples are amazing.' If you can feel yourself hitting the 'a' sound with too much force, then try using something called 'easy onset'. This is where you put a very slight 'h' sound in front of the vowel. The 'h' sound is used because when you say the letter your vocal folds are as wide apart as possible. By using the 'h' as the onset for the word, this encourages you to keep your vocal folds open and relaxed as you say the vowel sound as well.

Now try saying the sentence again, but this time with a very slight 'h' sound in front of each word. 'H-Apples h-are h-amazing.' See if you can feel the difference in the way that your vocal folds are working. You should feel a softer, more open quality to the sound.

Playing with Pronunciation

As well as being precise with your pronunciation, you can have some fun by playing around with different ways of pronouncing what you say. This will increase the sense of engagement for your students and it can be a lot of fun for the teacher as well. You might:

- ✓ Stretch some words like chewing gum, pulling out the individual syllables so that they create a longer sound.
- ✓ Put on a 'character voice' as you read the dialogue sections within a story.
- ✓ Figure out what kind of 'voice' an animal character in a story would have, getting your children to give their ideas as well.
- ✓ Play around with different ways of pronouncing words – in an accent, with different 'voices', at a different pitch, and so on.

Encourage your students to think about how your/their pronunciation of words can impact on what other people think about them. Help them understand why it is useful and important to use different vocal sounds and tones in different situations – formal, informal, school, home, the playground, and so on.

Using Emphasis

Pronunciation is about the way we say the individual words, but it is also about the emphasis that we put on each individual word within a sentence. By putting emphasis on specific parts of a sentence, you can completely change the meaning or purpose of what you are saying. It's all about being precise in your pronunciation – about getting across the specific message you had intended to communicate.

Let's have a look at how this works, by using a simple sentence that most teachers will have used in their classrooms at some point. Notice how the meaning can change almost totally, depending on the stresses the speaker uses. The sentence is: 'I didn't say you could do that.'

- ✓ If you were to say: '*I* didn't say you could do that', you are suggesting that someone else said they could, but that it just wasn't you.
- ✓ If you were to say: 'I *didn't* say you could do that', you are saying that they really shouldn't be doing it, that you definitely didn't give them permission to do it.
- ✓ If you were to say: 'I didn't say *you* could do that', you are saying that maybe someone else can do it, but that particular person definitely can't.
- ✓ And if you were to say: 'I didn't say you could do *that*', you make whatever 'that' is sound pretty awful.

The Fourth P:

Projection

The Fourth P: Projection

The ability to project your voice is vital for you as a teacher, and never more so than when you have to teach in a large open space, or in the outdoors. If you teach a subject such as physical education or drama at secondary school level, or if you regularly run sessions in a hall or a gym, it's especially vital that you understand how to project your voice properly.

Be aware of the acoustics of the room or rooms you teach in. Some spaces will dampen or suck up the sound of your voice, while other rooms will help you project your voice. Some rooms create an echo that is very disconcerting and distracting for both you and for the children. If you teach in a room with very difficult acoustics, ask your school leaders whether they could invest in a voice amplification system.

Remember, what we might consider a problem with students being able to *hear* is sometimes actually a problem with students being able to *listen*. As well as thinking about projecting your voice more clearly, consider whether your students need to learn to listen better, and also be *encouraged* to listen better. This can be done both through the way you use your voice and the way you use your body. For instance, sometimes a very quiet voice will encourage better listening from a class. Equally, you can give many classroom signals in a non-verbal way, thus doing away with the need to project your voice at all.

Voice projection is made up of three key elements:

✓   the way that you breathe;
✓   the amount of resonance you achieve; and
✓   the pitch of your voice.

Breath

In order to 'project' your voice, you need to increase the volume of the sound that you make. To do this, you must increase the amount of air coming from your lungs, or in other words, the amount of breath that is coming out of your body. When you increase the flow of air, this increases the air pressure under the vocal folds, which in turn increases the volume of your voice.

However, it's often the case that teachers 'force' a louder sound by using the larynx, rather than using breath to increase the projection of their voices. If you find that the muscles in your neck and throat tense up when you try to project your voice, then you are likely to be forcing your larynx rather than using an increased pressure of air.

For your breath to flow well, it's important that your posture is good, that your neck and shoulder muscles are relaxed, and that your head is well aligned with your spine. There is advice on good posture and breathing in section six of this book.

Resonance

Resonators are the 'speakers' in your head. Your vocal sound needs to vibrate around the spaces inside your head to create a louder sound, that can project right to the back of the teaching space. If your nose is blocked you can't resonate as well: this is why it's important to avoid speaking too much when you have a cold. The exercise below demonstrates this fact very neatly.

TRY THIS: Use your thumb and forefinger to pinch your nose together, then say the following sentence: 'Mighty mouse made many mistakes.' Now say it again, but this time without pinching your nose together. You will notice a clear difference in the strength of the sound that you can make without a blocked nose.

In order to increase the volume of what you're saying, you must allow the sound to resonate around your head as it comes out of your body. A good way to do this is to imagine the bones and skin in your head/face vibrating as you speak. (Try humming for a few seconds and you should be able to feel this happening.) Always avoid using your throat muscles to try and make your voice sound louder. This 'throat squeeze' is damaging to your voice, and it is also very ineffective in making the volume louder.

It can help to think of your voice as a physical object - one that you can literally hold in your hand, like a stone. As you project your voice, imagine yourself 'throwing' the stone towards the person who is listening. The exercise below is useful for helping you to understand how this feels.

TRY THIS: This makes a great activity for a staff training session on voice usage, and you can also do it with a friend instead. Ask the staff to get into pairs, and then to go and stand in two straight lines along the length of the room. Each person should face their partner, about a body's width apart. Explain to the staff that they are going to recite the nursery rhyme, 'Twinkle, Twinkle Little Star'. (You might want to quickly go through the words for anyone who doesn't have children of their own.)

Each person takes it in turn to say one line each. So, the first person says 'Twinkle, twinkle, little star', the second person says 'How I wonder what you are', and so on. Between each line, both people pause to take one step back, away from each other, so that by the end of the nursery rhyme they are far apart. The further apart they move, the more they need to project their voices. Ask them to do this by imagining they are throwing a stone towards their partners.

Pitch

We all have an optimum pitch level for projecting our voices: this is usually at a slightly lower pitch than our normal speaking voices. Look at the advice on pitch in the first section of this book to explore more on this fascinating subject. Remember that good breathing and a relaxed posture will ensure that you achieve the very best level of pitch for your students.

TRY THIS: Put your hand on your chest and make a long 'oooh' sound. Start with a high pitch, then gradually drop the pitch until it is as low as you can comfortably make it. As you do this exercise, feel how the vibrations in your hand increase or decrease. When the vibrations are at their fastest, this indicates your optimum pitch for the best quality of projection.

Projecting or Shouting

There is a big difference between projecting your voice and shouting. When you project your voice, your aim is to get your voice to travel further and reach the students more effectively, in a relaxed and comfortable way. When you shout, your aim is to increase the volume and get your students to listen. Typically you will shout because you want your students to know that you are angry or upset with them.

Most teachers will end up shouting at a class at some point in their careers (unless you are very calm and have high levels of self control). If you're in a very difficult school, you might find yourself doing this more regularly than you had hoped to.

There are a number of problems with shouting in the classroom context:

✘ It can be damaging for your voice, because when we shout we often do it with the 'throat squeeze' described previously, rather than by increasing the airflow from our lungs.

✘ Most teachers shout at a time when they are already angry. Those angry emotions tend to mean that the teacher's body is already tense, and this impacts on the quality of voice usage.

✘ Shouting very rarely works long-term to improve behaviour. Sometimes it doesn't even work at the moment it is used.

✘ There is very little that is more stressful in the classroom than a group of students who ignore you *even when you shout at them!*

Sometimes, you will need to raise your voice within your classroom for a very good and sensible reason. It could be that you need to stop a child immediately because he is doing something dangerous, or perhaps you need to show the class that they have pushed you far enough with their behaviour, and that their learning is being affected. The key is to raise your voice *from a position of emotional control* rather than *from a position of anger.*

When you do feel that you need to raise your voice:

✓ Think rationally for a moment – is raising my voice going to help in this particular situation? Is there something else I could try instead?

✓ Take a moment to ensure that your body is free of tension and that you have taken a good deep breath.

✓ Remember to 'throw' your voice across the space, as though it is a physical object.

✓ Keep in mind that vowel sounds travel through the air more easily and more freely than consonants. You might start with an 'oy' or an 'eh' to gain the children's attention.

✓ As you throw your voice towards the students, feel the breath resonating within your face, and helping you to project the sound.

The Fifth P:

Purpose

The Fifth P: Purpose

There is always a reason *why* you use your voice within your classroom: you speak because you are trying to achieve something specific. For instance, you might want to explain a new skill to the students, you might need to ask them to think about their behaviour, or perhaps you want to praise a child for very good work. The vocal and linguistic techniques that you use will vary according to what you are hoping to achieve when you speak. By analysing what these techniques are, you will be able to communicate more effectively, and you are more likely to achieve your intended purpose.

Purpose and Voice Usage

By looking at some of the purposes why we might use speech in the classroom, we can think about how best to achieve those aims. Remember that speaking on its own is one of the most inefficient ways to help children learn. Incorporate visual input, bounce the thinking backwards and forwards between yourself and the children, gather everyone's ideas, rather than simply telling the class. Aim for a limited amount of teacher talk: no more than the students' age plus two, as an absolute maximum at any one time.

Here are some different potential purposes, and some advice on the kinds of verbal and non-verbal techniques that will help you achieve them:

✓ **To instruct:** When you are giving instructions, use language that suggests some form of sequencing, so that your children can understand the various steps in the process. You might use 'first ... next ... finally', you might try 'first ... second ... third', you might use '(a) ...

(b) ... (c)'. Limit the number of verbal instructions you give at any one time, to ensure that your students actually remember what you want them to do. Back-up your instructions with visual input, for instance by drawing an image on your board for each step of the process.

✓ **To explain:** Explanations work best when the speaker's tone of voice is calm and low-key. Don't distract your listener from your explanation by using too much vocal tone. Use vocabulary that suits the ability level of the students, stretching them *just a little bit beyond* where they are at the moment. Introduce new key words carefully, giving a visual reference and talking about words with similar meanings, so that the children have something to 'grab onto' as you give your verbal explanation.

✓ **To engage:** When your purpose is to engage your children, think about the kind of vocabulary you use. Words like 'exciting' or 'fascinating' or 'interesting' will encourage them to engage with you and the subject. Use your most passionate voice to try and persuade your children that this particular topic/subject/skill is really worthwhile. You have to be genuine about what you say, though, so that you sound authentic. Children are very sensitive to whether a teacher's tone of voice matches his or her body language.

✓ **To inspire:** When your aim is to inspire your children, you'll need to get your body involved, along with your voice. Use your arms to gesticulate, and to show the sense of passion and energy you feel about this subject. Again, authenticity is key – if you want to inspire, you've got to *feel* inspired by what you are teaching. Find something within every subject or topic that triggers that feeling of enthusiasm within you.

39

✓ **To inform:** When you speak to inform your class about something, use straightforward language. Give the appropriate amount of detail – not so much that the students 'tune out', but not so little that you fail to stretch their understanding. Consider the 5W+H questions: who, what, why, when, where and how. It can work well to use vocal 'bullet points', going through a list of points and giving brief details about each one. Back up what you say with visual input, for instance, asking the students to note down the key ideas on a mini whiteboard.

✓ **To describe:** When you're describing something for the class, your language can become more flowery, and your voice can become much richer. Use imagery within what you say: incorporate metaphors, personification, allusions, and inference. Include sensory input as well, thinking about how you can bring the children's senses to life, by thinking about what they might see, hear, taste, smell and feel as you talk (in their imaginations, or in reality, depending on the topic).

✓ **To encourage:** Encouragement is often done one-to-one with a child, and it requires a warm tone of voice. If you believe that your students can achieve their best, then this will come through in the encouraging quality of your vocal tone. Use praise in a specific, focused way – say 'I really love the way you've used the colour red to add symbolism to your story', rather than 'That's a great piece of writing.' When you want to encourage the whole class, incorporate the vocabulary of targets into what you say – 'I just know you can all finish this activity in 3 minutes …'.

✓ **To control:** When you need to control the learning or (more often) the behaviour of a class or a child, use a rational, dispassionate and unemotional voice. Remove as much tone from your voice as you can. State what you want as a straightforward choice – if you choose to behave badly, then you will force me to apply this sanction, if you choose to behave as I wish, then all will be well. Refuse to get drawn into pointless debates and discussions – this is a waste of everyone's time. Be clear about what you want, by making statements, rather than using questions. So, you would say 'I need you to sit down now, thanks', rather than 'Why are you wandering around the room?'

Clarity of Purpose

It's important that your students understand exactly what you are explaining to them, or precisely what it is that you want them to do. This is a lot harder to achieve than it might at first sound. There are various reasons why it's hard to achieve clarity of purpose, and ensure clear understanding, when we are speaking:

✓ When we talk, we use figures of speech, or allusions, or imagery, or emphasis, or inference (often in a subconscious way). The purpose of what we are saying can easily get hidden behind a wall of tricky language, unless we think carefully about how we use our voices.

✓ Meaning is often shrouded in layers of ambiguity, or hidden behind visual imagery or figures of speech. For instance, you might use a saying such as 'it's a no-brainer' or 'get over yourself'. Whether a listener understands will depend on whether they have come across these phrases before or not.

✓ The meaning of language changes over time, so that words in common usage in one decade have fallen out of use or changed their meaning in the next. Language use also varies from region to region, and from culture to culture, so that even when two areas speak the same language, certain phrases or sayings will not transfer between the two.

✓ Interestingly, young people will often use the ever-changing nature of language to exclude adults from conversations they don't want them to understand. They will appropriate a word, and make it their own, often by subverting what the adults mean when they say it.

✓ Young children don't yet have the knowledge, or 'language base' to 'fill in the gaps' that we tend to leave when we talk. Some children's 'language base' is very poorly developed and they will find it hard to make any sense at all of what you are saying.

✓ Not all of your students are necessarily listening to every single word that you say, every single moment of the day. Some students find it much harder than others to gather meaning from speech. This is particularly so for those children who struggle with holding speech in their memories, or who have trouble in discriminating between spoken sounds.

To ensure clarity of purpose when you speak in your classroom:

✓ Don't use a big word if a small one will do. It's particularly important not to use long or complicated sounding words just because they make you feel clever.

✓ At the same time, introduce more complex vocabulary to stretch your students and to help them develop a wider vocabulary. A good way to do this is to say the same thing several times, but using a different word each time. For instance, 'I want you to pick out any bits of the story where it's not clear what the author is saying' could also be expressed as 'So, I'm looking for examples of ambiguity within the text.'

✓ Avoid using figures of speech, particularly if you work with students who have English as an additional language. Hear yourself as you talk, and try and 'catch yourself' using any phrases that don't lend themselves to easy understanding by second language learners.

The Sixth P:

Posture

The Sixth P: Posture

Your posture – the way that you stand and hold your body – has a direct impact on the quality of the sound of your voice. Ideally you want your vocal sound to travel freely out of your body on a breath, without being constricted or constrained by any muscular tension within your body. If your posture is strained, or tense, or cramped up, this will affect the quality of your vocal sound. It may also make you sound worried and stressed to your students.

Breath is what powers your voice. Breath vibrates the vocal folds, and the sound this creates then resonates around the spaces in your throat, mouth, nose and, to some extent, your chest. Good posture leads to good breathing, and good breathing leads to good voice production. If you stand tall and relaxed, the breath/sound can come out of your body freely. If you breathe well, from your diaphragm, your body will feel energised, relaxed and alert.

We all hold a certain amount of tension within our bodies. You need to figure out which parts of your body are tense, and how you might dissipate this tension. Often, people hold their tension in their neck or their shoulders (although for some people it can be somewhere completely unexpected, such as in the right hand). The exercise explained below will help you figure out where in your body the tension lies.

TRY THIS: Stand in an open space to try the exercise given below. This exercise helps you understand what 'good' posture feels like. You might like to try it with your students as well – often they carry a surprisingly large amount of tension in their bodies. I find that this activity works best if you close your eyes and really focus on feeling the various parts of your body, without any visual distractions.

✓ First, get into a good symmetrical starting position. Stand with your feet slightly apart, so that they are directly below your hips. Make sure that your feet are flat on the ground. Let your hands hang down loosely by your sides, relaxing your shoulders. Now you're ready to begin.

✓ First, picture your head being held high and relaxed on top of your spine. Imagine a small string attached towards the back of your head, which gently pulls your head and spine upwards and very slightly forwards, lengthening your entire body. Keep your chin slightly down, rather than 'leading' with this part of your face. If you visualise a slight upwards tug on the string at the back of your head, you should find the correct posture naturally.

✓ Feel your shoulders drop down towards the ground: don't push them down but just let gravity pull them down naturally. Allow your elbow joints to loosen and open – people often hold their tension in the crook of their elbows, keeping their arms very slightly bent and tense at all times. Think about your hands as well – are your fingers relaxed and loose, or are they tense and curled up?

✓ Now imagine your back opening out and widening, as though the two sides of your rib cage are gently moving apart. Check your shoulders again just to make sure that no tension has crept in. Allow yourself to take several deep breaths, feeling your rib cage expand on the 'in' breath and deflate on the 'out' breath. With each 'out' breath, imagine the tension flowing out of your body.

✓ Next check for tension in your legs. Are your knees 'locked' back and tight? If they are, gently loosen them so that your knees are relaxed and just very slightly bent.

✓ Finally, feel your feet firmly on the ground. Imagine that gravity is holding you to the ground, giving you a sense of 'weight'. At the same time, imagine your body still lifting upwards and away from the floor.

Top Tips on Classroom Posture

You need to keep your head, neck and spine well aligned, so that your voice can resonate around all of the cavities within your skull. As the breath/voice comes out of your mouth, imagine it filling up all those internal spaces with sound. This will create a good tonal quality and a well-rounded sound. Imagine the sound being projected towards the listener, through the front of your face.

Bad habits will often creep into your posture over time – you won't necessarily spot each bad habit as it forms, but after a while you might notice that your shoulders are always sore, or that your back tends to ache after a day at school. Try to become ever more aware of your posture, particularly those subconscious aspects of the way you use your body.

Here are some key ideas and thoughts about your posture in the classroom:

✓ Teachers often push their face and chin forwards, because they feel subconsciously that this might help their voice reach the back of a classroom. However, doing this cramps up the larynx and makes voice production harder rather than easier. Remember that small string just towards the back of your head: feel it lifting your head upwards and very slightly forwards, while keeping your chin relaxed.

✓ Make sure that you turn to your class when you want to address them. It's tempting to talk when you are facing the board, but your vocal sound will not carry in the right direction if you do this.

✓ If you find it hard to retain a relaxed posture when the students are watching you, then sometimes try teaching from the back of the room. Ask your students to keep their faces forwards, focusing on what you are saying rather than feeling the need to look at you.

✓ Watch your overall body language. Think about the messages that you send with different body postures. For instance what does it say to the children if you cross your arms or put your hands on your hips?

✓ Whenever you feel yourself getting tense about your students' behaviour, and you want to talk to the class about the problem, always check your body for good posture first. Take a few breaths to ensure that you speak in a calm, measured way and with an appropriately pitched vocal sound.

TRY THIS: Film yourself teaching your class, then afterwards watch the film back but with the sound turned down. See if you can spot where in your body you hold your tension. Do you notice yourself developing any bad postural habits, for instance jutting your chin forwards to 'reach' the back of the classroom?

Breath and the Voice

The way that you breathe has a direct impact on the quality of your vocal sound, and on how well you can sustain vocal production. It's important to be conscious of your breath, and to understand how breath works to create your voice. Remember, it's the out breath that vibrates your vocal folds and resonates around your head and neck on its way out of your body.

Here are some top tips about effective breathing for voice production:

- ✓ Breathe in fairly quickly and silently, using your diaphragm muscles. Your chest and shoulders should move very little as you breathe in.
- ✓ Focus on the out breath, because this is what powers your speech. You don't need to think about breathing in, because this happens automatically.
- ✓ As soon as you feel yourself about to run out of breath, pause to take an in-breath, before you continue to speak.
- ✓ Control your supply of air according to the length of phrase you want to use. When you breathe in, aim to take in enough air for the entire phrase.
- ✓ Don't squeeze out those last few words if you've run out of breath – pause and breathe in again before you speak.

TRY THIS: Read the phrases below, one at a time, taking one breath in before you say each phrase. Notice how it becomes harder for you to sustain a good quality vocal sound, as the phrases get longer. Which length of phrase is most appropriate for you?

- ✓ *I love teaching.*
- ✓ *I love teaching very much.*
- ✓ *I love teaching very much because of the children.*
- ✓ *I love teaching very much because of the children and because I love my subject.*
- ✓ *I love teaching very much because of the children and because I love my subject, but it is hard work.*
- ✓ *I love teaching very much because of the children and because I love my subject, but it is hard work and I do need my holidays.*

The Seventh P:

Protection

The Seventh P: Protection

As a teacher, your voice is your most valuable tool: without it, you cannot do your job. If you want to stay in the profession for any length of time, then you simply must learn how to use your voice properly. You must also understand how to protect your voice from damage, because it is all too easy to strain or damage it through incorrect usage. Amazingly, a teacher's vocal folds have to vibrate up to one million times a day in the classroom. It's obviously really important, therefore, that you understand how to use your voice correctly.

Interestingly, studies have shown that where a teacher's voice is impaired, this makes it harder for the students to understand what is being said. This effect is particularly pronounced for those children who have English as an additional language, for those children with learning or behavioural difficulties, and for those with a physical hearing impairment. So, not only must you protect your voice for your own sake, but you must also protect it to ensure that effective teaching and learning can happen in your classroom for all your children.

Teachers are much more likely that those in other professions to have problems with their voices. There are a number of reasons for this:

✗ Teachers make heavy use of their voices, on a daily basis, and don't have much time to recover between one school day and the next.

✗ Teachers are often required to project their voices quite a distance, or to speak over a variety of background noises.

✗ Teachers are exposed to a whole host of different germs and viruses, many of which can affect their voices in a negative way.

✗ The air in classrooms and schools can be irritating to the voice. This might be because of atmospheric pollutants that are present (dust or chemicals), or because the air is particularly dry.

✗ The acoustics found within teaching spaces are sometimes very poor. This is particularly the case with open teaching spaces such as gymnasiums and halls.

✗ The quality of voice training given during teacher education is very varied. Teachers often report receiving no specific voice training at all.

Non-Verbal Communication

Most teachers would admit to one very bad habit when it comes to protecting their voices: that they have a tendency to talk more than is absolutely necessary. You want to get the facts, information, ideas, thinking, skills, expectations over to the class, so you use your voice to tell the children – it feels like the quickest and most efficient method. Ironically, when the teacher uses too much talk, the children tend to take less information in. Similarly, teacher talk is not necessarily the best method for effective learning.

Use non-verbal ways to communicate with your class, whenever you can. These methods are particularly useful for classroom and behaviour management. For instance, you could:

✓ Write a message to the class on the board;

✓ Hold up a hand to show the children that you are waiting for quiet;

✓ Flick the lights off and on to get the class's attention;

✓ Ring a bell to call the class back to you.

There are many other non-verbal methods of communication you can use with your class. The only limit, really, is your imagination. I met one primary school teacher recently who had trained his children to respond to various different tunes played on a xylophone. He had a tune for tidying up, another for lining up to go to assembly, another for when he wanted the children's silent attention, and so on. It's a very effective idea and the perfect 'voice free' classroom management solution.

Protecting your Voice

To protect your voice you need to develop good habits around your voice usage, both in terms of the way you use it physically, and also in terms of how you use it pedagogically. You need to become knowledgeable about how you *should* use your voice, and conscious about how you *do* use your voice. Make it a priority for yourself to do this, because once you get into bad vocal habits these can be very hard to break.

To protect your voice from a physical perspective:

✓ Try not to clear your throat before speaking. This very quickly becomes a bad vocal habit and it is potentially damaging to your voice. Instead, swallow once before speaking or sip some water to clear your vocal sound.

✓ Warm up your voice before you begin teaching for the day, either before lessons begin, or with your children (see the next section for some vocal warm-up ideas).

✓ Drink sips of water throughout the day, particularly when it is dry or dusty. Avoid too much tea or coffee as this can be dehydrating. Smoking is obviously bad for your voice as well.

✓ When you have a cold or a respiratory virus, plan activities that require little or no speaking, so that you can rest your voice.

✓ If you regularly struggle with voice usage, or if you notice any change to the sound of your voice, visit your GP and ask for a referral to an ENT specialist. Your school could also support you by setting up some form of amplification in your classroom.

To protect your voice from the perspective of teaching and learning, and behaviour/classroom management:

✓ Move in close to a child to talk to him or her, whether it's about learning or about behaviour. Train yourself *never* to call across the room if you can possibly avoid it. If you do have to call across the room, use the correct projection techniques, as explained in the fourth section of this book.

✓ Try your very hardest to incorporate a period of time into each school day when you do not speak at all. For the most impact on your vocal health, this break should preferably be around 20-30 minutes. You might sit without speaking during your lunch break; equally you might plan a vocal break within your daily teaching schedule. For instance, you could set a silent, individual task within a lesson.

✓ Arrange your classroom layout so that any students who might need extra vocal attention are close to the front. This means that you don't have to raise your voice to give them the extra attention they need.

✓ Close your classroom doors and windows, to minimise the chance of background noise entering from other rooms or from the corridors. If you prefer to use an 'open door' policy, then you could close the door just for those parts of the lesson where you will be doing a lot of speaking.

✓ Create a 'quiet room' ethos, and refuse point blank to talk over background noise or chatter. Prioritise your own vocal health and train yourself to be a 'no shouting' teacher.

✓ Be very firm about your expectation that the children will fall silent when you need them to. Set this as a 'non-negotiable' right from the start.

✓ If you teach classes with very challenging behaviour, who simply refuse to fall silent for you, then refuse to talk over them in turn. Remember, it is your vocal health (and consequently your career) at stake. Use non-verbal methods to teach these classes in the short term (worksheets, writing tasks on the board, individual attention for those who want to learn). Ask your line manager for support in getting the silence you need.

Vocal Warm-ups

Just as you would warm-up your body at the start of an exercise class, so you should do a warm-up for your voice at the start of each school day. Remember, your use of voice is a *physical* part of your teaching technique: by warming up, you give your voice the priority it deserves.

✓ At primary school level, you could do some warm-ups along with your class, for instance, by starting each day with a few songs or some tongue twisters. Here are a few to get you started: 'Cheerful children chant charming

Printed in Great Britain
by Amazon